I AM A LOTUS

A book on mindfulness, meditation and reflection to become a lotus in mind and body

Anu Sehgal

Diah Chakraborty

Eternal Tree Books

I am a lotus.
From the depths of the muddy, murky waters I rise.
I persist and I prevail despite my circumstances.
When you emerge from difficult situations,
You become me.

I am a lotus.
My petals blossom white, pink, red, yellow, purple, and blue,
Each color as unique and beautiful as I am.
When you embrace your differences and shine on,
You become me.

I am a lotus.
My roots, my leaves, and my stem work in harmony with each other to keep me afloat and alive.
When you work harmoniously,
You become me.

I am a lotus.
I open every morning as the sun rises,
Setting my intention for the day and everything I am supposed to do.
When you wake up every morning and do your duty,
You become me.

I am a lotus.

I close every evening when the sun sets.

To rest, repair, and regain my strength.

When you end the day in gratitude,

You become me.

I am a lotus.
I rebloom every morning
Starting each day fresh with
determination and a smile.
When you keep up with your goals,
You become me.

I am a lotus.
I am a seat for the divine,
A symbol of wisdom, strength, and compassion.
When you spread goodness around you,
You become me.

I am a lotus.
My seeds spread beauty everywhere I go,
Bringing happiness to those around me.
When you spread your love and knowledge,
You become me.

I am a lotus.
Every part of me is consumed—
    I nourish, delight, and satiate those
    who find me.
    When you give back to the universe,
    You become me.

I am a lotus.

I am a symbol of peace, purity, and persistence.

I spread joy, love, and hope.

When you discover your inner strength,

You become me.

Author's Note

The lotus flower, known as Kamal in Hindi, encompassed our lives literally and figuratively as I grew up in India. One could find the flower in local ponds on a hot summer day, in temples adorning the thrones and statues of gods and goddesses, in architecture and art—commonly being the core of many designs and structures—in clothing adorning jewelry and henna designs with its symmetry and beauty, and in the foods we ate. Different parts of the plant are nourishing and delicious. Additionally, it played a significant role in dances and yoga. There are several references to Padma in mudras, asanas, and abhinayas.

To me, the lotus flower was magical, divine, and uplifting. Through my book, *I Am a Lotus*, I aim to share more about this angelic flower that has existed for centuries—revered and celebrated by several cultures and religions. I want the lotus to serve as an inspiration to children all over the world.

Become a Lotus

Padmasana (puhd-mah-suh-nuh)

Padmasana, or Lotus Pose, holds a pivotal role in yoga practice as a foundational pose. Derived from the Sanskrit word "padma," meaning lotus, the asana mimics the graceful shape of a lotus flower when performed. Serving as the primary seat for meditation, this seated posture offers numerous physical and energetic benefits. It enhances circulation in the lumbar spine, stretches the ankles and legs, promotes flexibility in the hips, and it promotes a profound sense of stability and connection, leaving practitioners with a deep-rooted and centered feeling.

Steps:

1. First sit on the ground with legs extended.
2. Place the right foot on the left thigh and the left foot on the right thigh.
3. Place the left hand on the left knee and the right hand on the right knee.
4. Keep the spine and head in a straight line.
5. Close your eyes and meditate.

Padma Mudra (puhd-muh muud-rah)

Padma Mudra, or Lotus Seal, resembles a blossoming lotus; it honors our inner beauty and light, inspiring purity and perseverance. Representing the lotus flower floating above the muddy waters of desire, fear, and attachment, this mudra reminds us of the natural beauty of our soul and calms the mind. It is frequently used in various classical dance forms from India.

Steps:

1. Sit straight with legs crossed.
2. Bring your hands softly into Anjali Mudra (namaste) in front of the heart center.
3. Slowly unfurl your hands, resembling a lotus flower blossoming open. Keep the base of the hands together, along with the thumbs and little fingers. Allow the index, middle, and ring fingers to gently open.